MALAYAN ANIMAL LIFE

(M. W. F. Tweedie)

Portrait of an Agamid lizard,
Gonocephalus belli

MALAYAN
ANIMAL LIFE

M.W.F. TWEEDIE, M.A., F.Z.S.

J.L. HARRISON, M. Sc.

LONGMAN

LONGMAN MALAYSIA SDN. BERHAD
44 Jalan Ampang, Kuala Lumpur
67 Miri Road, Singapore 4

LONGMAN GROUP LTD
London

*Associated companies, branches and representatives
throughout the world*

First published 1954
Second edition 1965
Third edition 1970

ISBN 0 582 69449 3

PRINTED IN HONG KONG
BY DAI NIPPON PRINTING CO. (INTERNATIONAL) LTD.